A Simple Guide to the Spiritual Life

by

Mark Kurowski

A Simple Guide to the Spiritual Life

By Mark Kurowski

1221 Azalea Drive, Munster, IN, 46321
ISBN: 978-0-615-30729-9

LESSON 1

What is Spirituality?

Not a 'What,' a 'Who'

Spirituality is not a project. It is a relationship. Let me explain.

Have you ever wanted something but you couldn't put your finger on it? When our oldest child was a toddler, he used to walk into the kitchen dragging his little blanket behind him. He would stop, place his finger on his lips, look up at the cupboards, and say, "I want somethin'." Of course, what he was talking about was food, but we can use this analogy for the spiritual life.

We often walk through life doing various tasks but feel there really is no purpose or direction. Sometimes we even may go to a church looking for "somethin'" and not find it. But we know that there is a need within us to connect with something beyond ourselves. What is that something?

That "somethin'" outside ourselves which will fulfill us within is actually a Someone. That Someone is God. The Someone we speak of has characteristics and features that have been revealed over the centuries. God is a Spirit. We begin to live a spiritual life when we recognize that the yearning we are having is the yearning for a relationship with God, so spirituality is developing a relationship with God.

Have you ever called someone many times on the telephone

and never got a returned call? Are you not asking yourself at some point, "Is anyone home?" This feeling of anticipation and frustration is that yearning. You want to talk with someone, but you cannot make the connection.

The yearning is God calling you, working within you, and asking you to return the call. Spirituality is the recognition that there is someone calling within you. That call demands a response just like a friend who stands before you and asks a simple question deserves a response. The response to the Someone who is calling within is the spiritual life. The spiritual life is incorporating the methods of "returning the call" of God into your daily routine and into the way you think.

The fact that you have downloaded this paper or have purchased the book means that you have already begun to answer the call of God which has been at work in you. Answering that call of God within you will be the only way to satisfy the yearning within. Today, we will lay the foundation for your journey to the spiritual life. We will then take weeks at a time to begin your walk to a deeper spirituality. Fulfillment and companionship are waiting for you to take hold of what has already been done for you and is calling within you.

Make Time for the Spiritual Life

The first step toward a spiritual life is to make a time to answer that call of God. It is no different from keeping an appointment with a friend every day. It is sustaining, playful, friendly, serious, incomprehensible, and simple.

I know this sounds terribly simple, but what you need to do is decide on a time and keep it.

The next step is to come to terms with the fact that all of us must crawl before we walk. This will take a long duration of weeks and months, but small bits every day are the start. You will need to realize that spirituality is not like taking a bite out of a sandwich but it is more like sipping tea or fine wine. We will start with small steps that eventually build into a different life.

Like every relationship, there will be peaks and valleys and starts and stops. Be patient with yourself, it will happen. The wisdom that will guide you comes from the Letter of James 2:13, "Mercy triumphs over judgement." Have mercy on yourself. If you should fail at any point, be sure to start from where you left off. Do not be hard on yourself. It is all right to begin again without having to make up for lost time.

Assignment

Since we have decided to be patient with ourselves and set a time to answer God, we are now ready for our first assignment.

You will need to decide on the time of day your appointment is scheduled with God, a notebook, a Bible, a pen/pencil, a chair that will allow you to relax without falling asleep, and possibly a timer that does not make a ticking sound.

Every day, for the next week, take five minutes at your designated time to just think about how this feeling you are having is God calling out to you. Write down in a little notebook or on a pad of paper the thoughts that come into your head and heart. It can be absolutely anything you are thinking.

It is very helpful to write down those things that get in the way of thinking about this question, too. You should write down all the things that you have to do in the day before you start. Say the following small prayer before you begin:

A Prayer of Release

Lord, I offer you these tasks of my day.
Take them from me for this short while.
I know that you can handle them and will refine them.
Bless these things
and keep them from troubling my heart
while I spend this time with you.
I ask this through Christ, our Lord. Amen.

Now, trust that God will take care of the things on the page. You can enter into your time with God without preoccupation.

Set the timer for five minutes. Breathe deeply and release this breath slowly. Do this a few more times. Relax your body with every release of breath. Now, begin to think of how this calling within is a calling from God. What does it mean to you to be called by God? Does this bring you peace? Does it trouble you? What does it mean to you to finally understand that while you have been searching for God, he has been with you all the time? Write down your reflections.

Dig Deeper

Turn in your Bible to 1 Kings 19:11-18. If you do not have working knowledge of the books of the Bible, please do not let that deter you. Every Bible has a table of contents at the beginning. Please feel free to look up where 1 Kings is located. We are not interested in expertise, but we are interested in establishing a relationship with God.

1 Kings 19:11-18 is the famous story of the prophet Elijah encountering God on Mount Horeb. This is the great prophet Elijah, who has just been used by God to cause a drought, bring a widow's child back from the dead, confront King Ahab, triumph over the prophets of the false god Baal, and end the drought. This same great prophet now flees in fear from Queen Jezebel. Even with all that success, Elijah, the great prophet, runs to a mountain and is cowering in fear. In his fear he cries out to God for help.

Where does Elijah find God? Let's take a look.

Beginning in 1 Kings 19:11, we see that God is not in the great wind nor in the earthquake but in a very unexpected place. There are several translations of this passage, but the one that is most correct according to the scholars is in the New Revised Standard Version. God is found in "a sound of sheer silence." In years past this was translated, "in the still small voice," but it was in the silence that Elijah found God and found strength to face his foes.

The exercise that I have started you on today is one that has been practiced by spiritual seekers and monks for millennia.

It is the unlikely place of practicing silence where we find God. Practicing silence is the farthest thing from our modern minds. Turn off your cell phones, computers, email, big screen television sets, etc. I want you to begin listening for God in silence.

The only way to get beyond the Baals, or false gods, of our world is to just turn them off. Listen. To listen we need to contemplate something in order to embrace silence. Later, I will talk about how to "embrace the silence." For now we need to get into the habit of meeting God every day on our "holy mountain." We need to think about how it is that God loves us and is calling us.

Much like Elijah, you might be facing uncertain times right now, but I want you to hold onto that one time of day where you are spending five minutes with God in the "sheer silence."

Assignment: Begin Meditating

For those who want to move on from the five minutes of contemplation of how God is calling us, here are some pointers. Begin each prayer time by breathing deeply and exhaling. I first started by focusing on the name of Jesus in two syllables. I would breathe in and concentrate on saying in my mind as I inhaled "Je" and exhaling on "_sus." Take nice deep breaths.

Be sure to get into a comfortable position that is enough to relax, but not too comfortable so that you fall asleep. Loosen your belt or tight clothing and take a moment to write down all the things that could possibly interrupt your prayer time that you must remember, as I outlined before. Now, let's begin to get in touch with God..

Thomas Merton, the famous spiritual guide and monk of Abbey Gethsemani (a recommended pilgrimage site) said, "meditation is the launching pad of prayer." Let us then begin our time by moving from practicing silence to meditation. I have a watch that has a little alarm so I can set it to remind me to go at least ten minutes (at first, now it is to remind me not to go more than fifteen minutes). You can meditate on the name of "Jesus" and let all the tightness of your body flow out of you.
Then, as you are meditating, let the meditation on the name of Jesus take on a life of its own.

Expect Jesus to encounter you. Trust that the Someone who has been calling you is God and that it is through the God-man Jesus Christ that he is going to reach out to you today.

Be sure to have your notebook to write down all the things that might interfere with your prayer time. And enjoy being in the presence of God in the sheer sound of silence.
Peace be with you. (You respond by saying, "And also with you.")

LESSON 2

How do I begin to live the spiritual life?

How did you learn to tie your shoes, feed yourself, or say 'please' and 'thank you'? You learned from someone else.

We need someone to teach us to begin the Spiritual life. That is what brings you to a web page, a book, or a spiritual director. Seeking out others who have done it before is how we have learned the Spiritual life for millennia.

The Spiritual life is a relationship between us and a Spirit who is 'other.' It is a Spirit that is much more than our little spirits within us. It is a powerful life-giving Spirit called "The Holy Spirit." Although much joy may have been robbed from your previous introduction to the Holy Spirit, let us learn to tie our spiritual shoes one more time.

It is doing what does not come naturally to us that begins the spiritual life. We need to lose focus on ourselves and focus on another. The spiritual life begins when we start to focus on God instead of ourselves. Unfortunately, we have been consumed by the information age and its focus on talking to ourselves. How do we learn to talk with a powerful, mysterious and inward filling Spirit like God?

We learn from those who have spoken to God before.

How do we do such a thing? We first begin to set aside a time every day to listen to God. Setting aside time for God was the focus of the last little sketch. By this time, you have already set aside a time for God every day. Then we begin to learn how God let others talk to him.

These songs, in poem form, were given to us by people who had a long-standing relationship with God. They are filled with emotions that are similar to emotions we have everyday–we are double crossed by an enemy, we are rejoicing at a windfall of some kind, we are angry at those around us, we have settled a dispute, we are horribly misunderstood, we are in deep intimacy with God, we are lost and alone.

The Psalms are found almost in the middle of the Bible. The Psalms have been used for many years as instructional guides on how to talk and listen to God.

Because the Psalms are poetry, they speak mostly of how people feel when they are talking with God. They do not always reflect how God acts in the world. They mainly tell us how much latitude we have in speaking with the God who called us to himself.

For the second lesson, we are going to begin to hand over control of our spiritual lives to God by reading as many Psalms or as much of a Psalm[1] as our meditation time permits. Read a Psalm and focus on a word or phrase which will see you through your day. Read slowly with purpose.

---

[1]*Psalm 119, in particular, is a lot to read in one sitting. If you are up to it, go ahead, but remember we need to be patient with ourselves and take time to get into a spiritual life.

Meditate on the phrase that expresses how you want to talk with God today. Write it on a slip of paper and carry it with you today. Look at it throughout the day.

For "extra credit" look at the phrase you wrote down at 9am, 12n, 3pm, 6pm and 9pm. This will make your day holy and refocused on God instead of you.

Dig Deeper

The Psalms contain 150 songs which were written by people who wanted to become more spiritual by talking with God. They reflect a relationship with a being, a person. To live a spiritual life, we need to get out of ourselves and focus on someone else: God.

God does have a name. Jesus Christ said, "When the Spirit of truth comes, he will guide you into all the truth . . . for he will speak what he hears . . . he will take what is mine and declare it to you. All the Father has is mine . . . [the Spirit] will take what is mine and declare it to you."[2] God's name is "Father, Son and Holy Spirit": one name, one being, three persons. We can talk about that later, but the idea is to get to know God.

Here we see that the Spirit, who is God, will take what he hears from the Father (who is God), which is given through the Son (who is God) and proclaim it to you. Cool! It is a community with one substance: God. This mystical community speaks as one and works as one.

---

[2] John 16.12-15.

The Spirit has been calling you to start a spiritual relationship with God in a spiritual community. The Spiritual Community is a collection of the people who wrote the Psalms and who chant them today. Yes, I said "chant!" (See below) That Spiritual Community can teach you how to speak with God simply by reading the Psalms.

God has given you a way to talk with him: the Psalms.

The Psalms teach us how to talk to God. They are very free in their speaking. The Psalms teach us that we can talk with the Spirit in ways that are really very free. They are free because God is not canned, but is as free, playful and interesting as the people we meet. In fact he is even *more* interesting. God is open to listening to us whatever situation life brings us.

The one thing we often deny in our United States version of religion is that life can really stink sometimes. Life can be hard especially for the faithful. It seems if we cannot smile all of the time, then we are not being 'positive.' People will shy away from us when we are not positive all the time. Not so with those who wrote the Psalms!

Sometimes life is hard. And the people who wrote the Psalms tell us that they let God know about it:

Psalm 22 reads, "My God, my God, why have you forsaken me? Why are you so far from helping me, from the words of my groaning?" These are not the words of someone who has just had a happy experience. Of course, God is not far from this person, it just feels like he is. When we cannot hear God we often think he is far away. The fact that God called you to start a spiritual life is a sign that even when you didn't know him fully, he called you and is close to you. The Psalm writers also expressed other aspects of their relationship with God through the Psalms:

Amazement. Psalm 8 reads, "When I look at your heavens, the work of your fingers, the moon and the stars that you have established; what are human beings that you are mindful of them, mortals that you care for them?" This is a guy who has just looked out the window, had a cup of hot coffee (tea or whatever), took a deep breath and realized, "Wow! I've really got it made! God, how is it that you have come to bless me so!" (See Psalm 103, too.)

God's Reliability. Psalm 89 recounts the deeds that God has done for the people of the Psalms. I want you to know that since you recognized that you needed to recognize your spirituality, you are now a part of the wonderful history that the writer recounts in this Psalm. This history is now becoming your history.

Here is an outline from Claus Westermann's wonderful thick thinkers book *The Living Psalms* to guide you. Dig into the Psalms and begin talking with God throughout the day.

- Psalms of Praise (Thanksgiving Psalms): 30, 31:7-8 (19-24), 40:1-11, 66, 116, 138, 113, 33, 145, 29, 103, 104, 19, 148, 8, 139
- Psalms of Trust: (Psalm number only) 123, 126, 124, 4, 23, 73, 27.1-6, 62, 90, 46
- Psalms of God's Kingship: 72

- Psalms of Lament: 80, 44, 74, 79, 89, 83, 13, 6, 22, 51, 77, 102, 103
- Psalms of the Liturgy (Worship): 118, 24, 122
- Psalms of Blessing and Wisdom: 121, 1, 119

A Little Trip to Kentucky...

When I was writing a paper in Seminary, a strange twist of events led me to the monastery, Abbey Gethsemani, at Bardstown, KY. It is known as the place Thomas Merton, the great spiritual writer, lived and worked. I think it is even better because of the sermons Fr. Matthew gives.

The monks get up and sing at 3 a.m., 6 a.m., 9 a.m., 12n, 3 p.m., 6 p.m. and 8 p.m.! The lights are put out right away then. You have to really love God to get up at three in the morning to sing the Psalms to him!

Did I say sing? I sure did. I will get to that in a moment.

The monastic movement was a reform movement in the church. Whenever the church got too worldly, a community of people who wanted to radically follow Jesus Christ through the Holy Spirit would spring up. These communities are radical. The center of their existence is to worship Father, Son and Holy Spirit through Jesus Christ.

These folks, men and women, get up at a set time every day. For those at Abbey Gethsemani, it is near 3 a.m.. They sing the Psalms, pray together, worship together, listen to scripture being read, and then balance that with a life of work and self giving. More and more the monasteries are pushing their monks and nuns outside the walls to do the daily work required of them.

We are going to adopt and adapt their daily pattern of prayer which causes them to fulfill the scriptures to "Pray without ceasing."[3] Praying on the daily hours of three, six, nine, twelve, etc. helps them to do that. They pray on these hours because of their deep and abiding love for God. It may seem that they are giving more than getting, but their lives are a testimony to what a spiritual life is worth.

Now, those of us with families find it hard to leave them behind (and we shouldn't!). We can incorporate these hours of prayer in little bits into our lives. Those who do the extra credit will find that they are following a cycle of prayer called "The Daily Office".

---

[3]1 Thess. 5.17.

LESSON 3

How do I respond to God? Prayer, what is it? How do I pray?

Have you ever greeted someone and before you could finish your "hello" they said, "Good. And you?" What is even more maddening is that they are off to another subject before they have even acknowledged your existence.

Don't be frustrated. God puts up with this all of the time.

If you have been on the journey through the first two lessons. We have been listening for God and keeping silent. These are essential, but every communication requires listening and then response. What drives us crazy about the people who talk right over us is that they are ignoring us. We have been spending good time paying attention to God.

Look over your notebook. What are the things that have caught your attention in your silent time with God? What are the things that have shaped your days as you walked through them (remember the paper and praying at 6 a.m., 9 a.m., 12n, 3 p.m., 6 p.m., and 9 p.m.)? These are things that God has been whispering to you (or possibly shouting over to you!).

We now need to start to respond to God. We do that through prayer. Prayer is a thoughtful and deliberate conversation with God. In the first lesson we made time to have silence and meditate on God wanting us to be in relationship with him. This is concentrated listening which you have already been doing.

We read how other people spoke to God. You have done this with reading the Psalms. Now we need to pray. We do this by using what we have learned and adding something new, our own petitions (or requests).

Prayer is doing those first two steps, listening and reading how others prayed, and then we speak. We can speak silently in our hearts or out loud with our lips.

There are several patterns for prayer to help us. Depending upon who you are, how creative you want to be, and how much time you have, there are many forms from which to choose.

Briefly, use the Lord's Prayer as your guide. It starts with prayers for God's kingdom. This classic prayer moves to prayers that bring us closer to others. Finally, there are prayers for ourselves. We should begin our prayer with, "In the name of the Father, and of the Son, and of the Holy Spirit . . . " and then pray.

Dig Deeper

Jesus Christ said that we should baptize in "the name of the Father, and of the Son and of the Holy Spirit." Why would we do that? Why would we use this formula to start and end our prayer time?

Surely you know that if you call someone for a job interview and are referred by someone they know, you are more likely to get results. You say, "Cortland Starrett told me to call you." Because he knows Cortland Starrett, and knows he is a really good judge of character, the man on the other end of the phone is more likely to invite you in for an interview.

The Scriptural understanding of doing things "in the name" of someone comes from the sending of messengers when they had a message from a King. The messenger would go from one kingdom to another, stop, and say, "I come in the name of the King . . . " There was and is power in a name.

We pray in the name of the Father, Son and Holy Spirit because to become spiritual is to know God who is a Spirit. "Father, Son and Holy Spirit " is his name. To pray in this name is to appropriate the power, character, spirit and devotion of God. This appropriation of God's name gives us more upon which to rely than just ourselves. Appropriating God's name is shifting us into the mystical, spiritual, reality of eternity.

'Becoming Spiritual' means we are looking to enter the presence, power and excitement of being in relationship with the Spirit who is God. Considering that God is the one who created the complex universe with a simple spoken Word, we can trust that his name has power and mysterious depth. We enter this mysterious power by starting our prayer time with 'In the name of the Father, Son and Holy Spirit. Amen.'

Another Form of Prayer: The Collect

The "Collect" is not a collection. It is a form of prayer. The Collect basically 'collects' the theme of the service, the week, the person praying or the occasion of the Mass/worship service. Here is the Collect for the Second Week of Easter in the Book of Common Prayer and The

Liturgy of the Hours.

The Book of Common Prayer
Almighty and everlasting God,
who in the Paschal mystery
established the new covenant of reconciliation:
Grant that all who have been reborn into the fellowship of Christ's Body
may show forth in their lives what they profess by their faith;
through Jesus Christ our Lord,
who lives and reigns with you
and the Holy Spirit,
one God, for ever and ever. Amen.

The Liturgy of the Hours
God of mercy,
you wash away our sins in water,
you give us new birth in the Spirit,
and redeem us in the blood of Christ.
As we celebrate Christ's resurrection
increase our awareness of these blessings,
and renew your gift of life within us.
We ask this through our Lord Jesus Christ,
your Son,
who lives and reigns with you
and the Holy Spirit, one God,
for ever and ever. Amen.

These prayers have a basic form:
1. Address to God "Almighty and everlasting God . . . " or "God of mercy . . . "
2. Characteristic of God "who in the Paschal mystery . . . " or "you wash away . . . " (Something God has done)
3. The petition (or request) "Grant that all who . . . " or

"increase our awareness . . . "
4. The hoped for result "that all who have been . . . " or "renew your gifts . . . "
5. Final praise of God "through . . . who lives and reigns . . . Amen."

I will post on my website, http://www.MySpiritualAdvisor.com, the work of anyone who wants to try to write a Collect.* You can start simply if you want, but I encourage you to give it a try.

Assignment:
Before you begin, make a list of prayer petitions for the world, others and then ourselves.
Begin at your designated time and meditate for five minutes.
Read and meditate on a Psalm.
Pray the Lord's Prayer
Pray the petitions on your list
Close with "In the Name of the Father, and of the Son, and of the Holy Spirit. Amen."

LESSON 4

When should I pray? The rhythm of time and praying.

Really, now, you do the same things every day and every week don't you? If you are neat, you have developed a routine for keeping things tidy. If you are, uh, not so neat, you have a routine of where you put the pizza boxes in the room when you are done with them. The reason we have these habits is because they create a rhythm of life that is a great comfort to us. We probably have never thought of our lives as being rhythmic. But they are. There is a rhythm to everything.

We manage our relationships by the rhythm of time. I pick up my son every Tuesday for lunch from the bus stop. Every Tuesday night I meet with three other men to pray for our families and to encourage us to keep the spiritual life going. Every night my wife and I talk for about an hour about our children. This same rhythm of life for maintaining relationships is the same rhythm we use with our relationship with God.

The church took the hours at which the different events of Jesus' life led to his death and resurrection for the hours at which they should pray. These hours are 6 a.m., 9 a.m., 12 p.m., 3 p.m. and 6 p.m.. These hours are called the "daily office." I want you to take a moment today at each of these hours. Pray your regular prayer as close to 6 a.m. as possible and 12 noon. Then take little thirty second prayers at 9 a.m., 3 p.m. and 6 p.m. This keeping the rhythm of life is really becoming more spiritual.

"Becoming more spiritual" is more than just turning within ourselves and getting a good feeling for about ten minutes every day. Becoming more spiritual means we are being changed from within so that our view on life is different. To be more spiritual means that we are replacing bad habits with good ones. To be more spiritual means that we are getting our physical body more in line with what we say we believe and what we want to believe.

This is the wonderful thing about the Spirit, he gets within you and starts to challenge you to do things that you never thought you were capable of doing. Then the Spirit gives you the will, or the grace, to do the things he asks. The more you encounter the Spirit, the more you are changed. The more you are changed, the more you handle life in a more spiritual way.

This may not mean that you stop doing everything you don't like about yourself (as I can truly attest), but it does mean that your outlook on life will begin to change. If you are doing it right, there will be little changes throughout the day. When we start to see things differently, then our actions about what we see will change.

I hate to tell you this, but this process is called "moral formation." It means that the way you act (your moral action) is being formed by your view on life (your formation). I hate to tell you this because we usually associate "being moral" with being prudish and cool to others. Being moral couldn't be farther from being prudish and cool. Being moral is a life that is warm, open, and disciplined by our spirituality.

It is like learning to ride a bicycle. If you start to practice and you fall off, there are two choices: stop riding or keep trying until you get it right. This is the same with spiritual practices. We need to keep trying them to get them right. It is the consistency of practicing them that forms us.

Where riding a bicycle every day gives us skills at bike riding, praying every day gives us spiritual formation skills. When we pray at various times throughout the day, then we are constantly being formed and our way will be changed. The Lord, who is the Spirit, will encounter us and change us.
It is just that simple.

The more complicated stuff happens when we start to apply what we know to the tough areas of life. The formation of praying the "daily office," which is praying at 6, 9, 12, 3, 6 and bedtime, is the formation of becoming more like Christ. For that, we should Dig Deeper.

Dig Deeper
The rhythm of prayer times was set by the events of the life of the church and the events in the life of Christ. As I said earlier, the rhythm of time is how we maintain relationships.

The early church, and at least parts of the church over the millennia, was and is composed of people who actively love the Spirit continually. They do and did want to "pray without ceasing" as 1 Thessalonians 5.17 tells us to do.

To "pray without ceasing" is to maintain the relationship with God throughout the entire day. To do that, it is helpful to have checkpoints like a runner on a marathon has checkpoints to keep her on her path. These "checkpoints" are the hours of the day.

6 a.m., This is usually the time of sunrise. We pray the prayer I have introduced you to praying in Lessons One and Two. Don't change the time you set for your prayer time. Yet, this is the beginning of the day. It is when the Daystar rises. It is also the time when our Daystar rose from the dead. This event filled us with so much joy that we celebrate the resurrection of Jesus first thing every morning. It is important to start the day with the Resurrection in our hearts, on our minds and springing from our lips. Today is a day of new birth and renewal. The first order of prayer of the day celebrates this newness of life we find in a new day.

9 a.m. Most of us are at work at this time. This is the time when we can stop for a quick sixty second prayer and meditation at our desks or on the work floor. When we do, we remember that this is the time when Jesus Christ started his work on the Cross.[4] This is the hour they crucified Jesus Christ. We stop and say a prayer that our work will glorify God like Jesus Christ's self giving work glorified God on the Cross.

12 n. We are all taking a break from the daily grind at this time of day for lunch. This is the hour that Jesus Christ took a break from the world. It is the hour at which he breathed his last. At this moment we contemplate with a psalm, prayer, the Lord's Prayer/Our Father, and meditate on how Jesus was faithful until the end. Let us pray that we remain

---

[4]Matthew 27.45-50. Please read this.

faithful in the working world until the end of the day.

3 p.m. Here is when we are ready to fall asleep on the job. It is also the time that Joseph of Arimathea took careful time to place the body of Jesus in the tomb.[5] We can take sixty seconds to pray that we will take care to do our Lord justice with the rest of our workday. We also pray for the Spirit to carry us the rest of the way.

6 p.m. This was the prayer at the setting of the Sun. The lamps usually were lit in homes at this time. It is the time we remember to light the lamp of our hearts for the Spirit. We say we are sorry for the things we did that brought darkness into other people's lives to cleanse ourselves for the next day. We thank the Light of the World, Jesus Christ, for being in us and guiding us in the darkness.

All of these times keep us on course. Remember to be patient with yourselves. If we say these prayers it should have taken about 32 minutes out of our day total.

Get into the rhythm of time. Let it keep you dancing with the Spirit. We become more spiritual by keeping the rhythm of time. This rhythm keeps us in relationship by helping us focus on the Spirit who is constantly calling us.

These meditation prayers, sung by the religious, give us peace and prepare us for the encounter with the Holy Spirit. Purchase some Gregorian chant CDs after you have had a chance to spend this time praying.

---

[5]Matthew 27.57-61. Please read this.

Assignment

Pray at your usual prayer time as close to 6 a.m. and 12 n as possible and then short prayers at 9 a.m., 3 p.m. and 6 p.m.
We maintain our lives through a rhythm of time.
The rhythm helps us maintain our relationships.
Use the rhythm of time to maintain your relationship with the Spirit whose name is Father, Son and Holy Spirit.
We become more spiritual by keeping the rhythm which then changes you by making these prayer times important to your whole day.

LESSON 5

Material Gifts from God

When God wanted to save the world, he didn't send a spirit. When God wanted to save the world, he came in the form of a human being. This is the best example I can use to tell you what sacramentalism is and why it is important. Simply, Sacramentalism is the key to the spiritual life.

Sacramentalism is the belief that God works through physical things to affect our lives. What sacramentalism declares is that there is nothing outside of God's strength. There is no more of an ultimate spiritual declaration than this: God can use whatever he wants to speak to us, change us and work in our lives! God can use even physical elements transformed by his grace.

Genesis, the first book of the Bible, opens with the incredible declaration that God created the heavens and the earth. Since God is spiritual, this fact alone says something. Before we quote Scripture, it says that God, a spiritual being, can work to bring about physical change. This is a statement of incredible power and flexibility on God's part.

Then, when Genesis says, "God [spoke]," and things were created. This shows the power of God's spoken word. It opens up for us a whole world of possibilities as to what happens when the word of God is spoken over physical elements such as a body, oil, bread and wine.

The implication is that God's words spoken over us can

change us. We are physical bodies. This movement of the spoken re-creative power of God's word is an incredible thing to think about.

When you sit in church and listen to sermons and you realize that God is speaking through the speaker, then what they have to say is transformational. When a person speaks the word of God over the elements, the spiritual reality of God acting over those elements is beyond the limited scope of reason. God's power is beyond us. This fact is empowering.

The word spoken can bring about the change of wine into Christ's life giving blood and the bread into his sustaining body. When we ingest the God changed bread and wine, it changes our bodies, changes our souls.

When you have the pastor or priest pray over you and anoint you with oil, then you have the possibility of the oil being changed into a transformational agent. This means that God's power, re-creative power, can be given to those who are sick. God's power transforms their physical bodies by a spiritual presence in the physical reality.

When you have the pastor or priest stand before two people who declare the word of God at a marriage, then there is a transformational nature of the man and woman that makes more than just a contract-like marriage possible. Two people acknowledging the act of God in their relationship means that it is a transformational event. This means that you have the possibility of a man and a woman being transformed into spiritual realities that go beyond just physical realities through marriage.

All of these transformative things happen through the word of God, the Spiritual life, using the physical realities of our lives to achieve other worldly things. Bread and wine give Sustenance and Life. Vows give transformational marriage.

Sacramentalism is the belief that God is strong and mighty enough to work through physical elements to help us in our lives. This is why we can touch a Bible and read it through physical eyes and have our hearts changed in a physical and spiritual way.

The work of God through the physical also means that God cares not just about your spiritual being, but your physical well being, too. Take care of your body, exercise and pray. Take care to do good deeds with your body. Take care of yourself as a total being. God came to deliver you as a totally physical spiritual being.

Dig Deeper

It is no accident that when the world needed someone to bridge the gap between God and the people who were supposed to follow him that a human being emerged on the scene. Deliverance wasn't and isn't found only in a spiritual being. Deliverance is found in a transformational physical human being, Jesus Christ.

The Christian claim about Jesus is more than just that he was human. The claim is that the humanity he received from the Virgin Mary is tied to the divinity of the Second Person of the Trinity. The Second Person of the Trinity is "Son" of "Father, Son and Holy Spirit."

Why is this important? This coupling of the Spiritual "Son" and the humanity of "Mary" means that God is concerned with both your spiritual and physical well being. This spiritual working through the physical opens up all kinds of wonderful possibilities.

Possibility Number One: We can receive a spiritual act of membership through a physical means. This is Baptism.

Possibility Number Two: We can receive a physical presence of Christ within our bodies through a physical means. This is Holy Communion (also called "The Eucharist").

Possibility Number Three: We can receive a tangible physical act of forgiveness which simultaneously works a spiritual act of cleansing. This is Confession.

Possibility Number Four: We can receive a gift of the Holy Spirit later in life that urges us to continue in the faith which was proclaimed to us. This is Confirmation.

Possibility Number Five: We can have people who are called to a spiritual higher calling who serve as a means of Christ's presence among us. This is Ordination.

Possibility Number Six: We can have a spiritual union between people that is achieved through a physical joining. This is Marriage.

Possibility Number Seven: We can receive spiritual power for healing through a physical medium. This is Anointing of the Sick.

Assignment
Please read these passages on these days while thinking of the focus given for that passage. Then do the physical action encouraged by the spiritual message.

Monday: Read Genesis 1 (Out of nothing, the Spirit creates physical things and then gives them life.). Do something that gives someone a chance at life.

Tuesday: Read John 1.1-14 (Jesus Christ is the ultimate sacrament, God-man). Find a place to celebrate Holy Communion (Also, "the Eucharist.").

Wednesday: Read Jeremiah 31.31-34 (The promise of cleansing through Jesus Christ). Go clean up the side of a busy road nearest your home.

Thursday: Read Ezekiel 36.23-32 (The promise of cleansing through baptism, see also Romans 6). Go tidy an elderly person's yard today.

Friday: Read 1 Peter 3.18-22 (Baptism is what saves us through the Holy Spirit cleansing us). Give a donation to your local homeless shelter, or better, volunteer at your local homeless shelter.

Saturday: Read Luke 24.13-35 (The Eucharist is an encounter with Christ through the Bread). Go through your cupboards and give your best food to the local Food Bank.

Sunday: Read John 6.52-65 (The bread is his flesh and the wine is his blood) Go to worship today.

LESSON 6

Visual Aids Help Us

How do you learn? Are you aural dominant (you learn through listening)? Are you visual dominant (you learn through seeing things)?

Educators have discovered that we are all dominated by a certain way of learning. There is much work to teach us how to translate our education into our style of learning. Some of us learn better through pictures than we do through listening. Some of us do better through activities with our hands than through watching.

The point I am making is that for the early church, most of whom could not read, the primary form of learning and remembering during worship was through iconography. Iconography is the pictorial or symbolic representation of Christian ideas, persons, and history. Christians have never held that icons were God. Icons are a way to help people to get to know God and his ways.

Icons simply point us toward God and God toward us. Icons remind us of what we are to be concentrating on during our contemplation/meditation time. I recommend you visit the site that gave us St. Mark on the left. Go to http://www.iconofile.com to see Anne Pinkerton Davidson's work.

Use the icon to focus on the story it represents. Some Evangelicals drive around with the Fish on the back of their cars. That is an iconographic representation of the Greek acronym for "Jesus Christ Son of God." Those letters spell "ICHTHUS" pronounced "ikthoos." Ichthus is the same word for "fish." If those kind folks would take the fish off of their cars and put it in their prayer space in their homes, they could concentrate on it and meditate on it to help them focus during prayers.

It is just an incredible thought that God spoke and physical matter was brought to form out of nothing. The operative word in the creation passages is "said." "God said, let there be . . . and there was . . . "[6]

The world and God's creation works the same way. God is not permanently in a tree. God is not permanently in dirt. God is spirit and can use those things to communicate his grace to us through them, if he wants. The direction God keeps going is away from himself. By way of an explanation about pictures I will explain how God reaches out to you through icons.

Every picture has a focal point. When someone paints a picture, there is a spot on the canvas to which everyone's eye is drawn. The things around the focal point naturally draw the eye toward the focal point. Although this is true of a picture, you could look long and hard at a Christian icon all day and not find the focal point in the picture.

---

[6]Genesis 1. Please read the chapter and note how God activated creation.

Icons are made so that they convey God's grace. The focal point of an icon is not in the picture. The focal point of an icon is you, the viewer. The whole point is that God is reaching out to you through the message of the icon. The icon is a vehicle through which God is speaking.

Back in the olden days, there were plenty of icons in churches because they told a story to people who could not read. All the clauses of the Nicene creed are depicted in the twenty-two illustrations of F. Boesplug's Credo de Sienne (1985). These pictures depict the Creation, the Trinity, the Father as maker of heaven and earth, Jesus Christ ascended at the 'right hand of God,' and more. They are found in the choir stalls of a church in Siena, Italy.

Choirs in churches are places of prayer. As you pray the focus of the grace is on you. God is communicating to you. This is why iconographers go through extensive theological training. Iconographers will tell you that when they draw, they pray. Every stroke is a prayer that lasts and communicates to you.

Again, the point of an icon is to focus on you. You are to see the story of the icon and be touched by the grace it represents. The Crucifix is the greatest of all icons. The Crucifix reminds us of the scripture in Galatians 3.10-14 and continues proclaiming the Lord's death until he comes (1 Cor. 11.26).[7] I would recommend that you purchase a

---

[7]For all who rely on works of the law are under a curse; for it is written, "Cursed be everyone who does not abide by all things written in the Book of the Law, and do them." Now it is evident that no man

crucifix for every room in your house. Place it above your door, or place it in a place where you can look at it when you are in bed.

The process through which we use an icon during prayer time is to know what it depicts and meditate on that. Use the Crucifix for starters.

The Crucifix reminds us that the death of Christ paid for our sins. We know he suffered like we suffer by looking at the Crucifix.[8] The idea of his sacrifice for us comes home when we realize that in the Crucifixion Jesus died from having his arms stretched to the point that he could not breathe. It was death by suffocation. He was slowly being suffocated for three hours.

Knowing this we focus on the Crucifix like a pregnant woman focuses on a point in the room using natural childbirth methods. During this meditation, we may hear Christ saying to us, "I did this for you. I did this for you." We

---

is justified before God by the law; for "He who through faith is righteous shall live"; but the law does not rest on faith, for "He who does them shall live by them." Christ redeemed us from the curse of the law, having become a curse for us–for it is written, "Cursed be everyone one hangs on a tree"–that in Christ Jesus the blessing of Abraham might come upon the Gentiles, that we might receive the promise of the Spirit through faith."

1 Corinthians 11.26, "For as often as you eat this bread and drink this cup, you proclaim the Lord's death until he comes." The crucifix does the same thing. It proclaims the Lord's death until he comes again.

[8]See Hebrews 2.10-18.

realize what kind of a sacrifice was made for us and we enter into a communion with the Savior of the Universe at a deeper spiritual level.

We then begin to pray thanks for his offering for us. We begin to pray glory to God for his willingness to accept us. We who have sin are accepted into him who knew no sin. This happens in baptism. If we have been baptized, then we reclaim our baptism. If we have not been baptized, then we should seek out a church and enter the process for baptism. Baptized or not baptized, we can still pray and meditate in this way.

This process is why it is important for people who worship where there is a Crucifix to get there early and meditate.

Dig Deeper
There are certain standard symbols that tell us what is going on in an icon. For example, if there is a man with keys in his hands in the icon, then it is St. Peter. This a picture of what Jesus said in Matthew 16.19.

So it goes with icons: scripture, scripture everywhere! For evangelicals and charismatics, the key is interpreting the scene on the icon and then finding out that it is all scripture. The most prominent is the falling of the Holy Spirit upon the church at Pentecost.

Here are some other keys to reading icons:
Halo - There will be a halo around everyone who was and is holy in an icon. A halo with what would be a cross on it is the halo around Jesus Christ. A halo with a line coming from it are streams of light and represent the Father in heaven,

usually. Usually the beams are grouped in threes for "Father, Son, and Holy Spirit."
Circles - A circle represents completion and eternity. There is no beginning or end to a circle. Also, all things which are contained in a circle are complete and need nothing else.

Rays of Light - Rays of light usually depict the glory of God. Jesus Christ will have rays coming from his halo at times, but remember the halo of Christ has a cross impressed on it.

Dove - A dove represents the Holy Spirit. Usually you will see the dove descending upon people at Baptism and on Jesus at his Baptism.

Eight - There are sometimes windows in a Church with eight sides, eight panels, eight whatever. Eight is the symbol for the eight people saved through water on the Ark and the "eighth day" of the week when Jesus rose from the dead. It is a "new day" that is understood theologically as the day that we were saved by Christ in his resurrection. This is why baptismal fonts (places where people are baptized) have eight sides.

Sometimes eight is paired with six. The sixth day is Friday when Christ was crucified and the eighth day is the New Day of Easter and Resurrection.

Angels - Iconography of the medieval times loved angels. When you see angels blowing trumpets, you can be quite sure that this the Judgment Day when Christians go to heaven.

Twelve Men - Twelve men are usually the apostles of Jesus Christ. Each one may have something about them that is in

the icon. The "evangelists" or the writers of the Gospel are each depicted as having something about them that is in their icon. St. Mark's Icon on the home page is holding a pen and writing. It reminds us of the gift of the Gospel. It is copyrighted 1993 by Anne Pinkerton-Davidson.

Assignment

Use an icon during prayer time as described in the article.
Remember the following:
Icons are pictorial or symbolic representations of Christian ideas, persons and history.
They are not gods.
They help us to focus during prayer time.
They are a means through which the grace of God is given to us.
They have meaning that reminds us of the majesty of God.
Icons draw us toward God by having us as their focal point.

LESSON 7

How to Read and Understand the Bible

When David Koresh's compound in Waco, Texas was set on fire, the real issue was how the Bible was read. To become more spiritual, you need to read the Bible. How the Bible is interpreted by a faith community makes all the difference in your spiritual life.

David Koresh was a leader of a group of people called the "Branch Davidians". They believed that David Koresh was the incarnation of Jesus Christ who had come back to lead a violent end to the world and redemption for all who followed him. The government had a standoff with Koresh in his compound in Waco, Texas. This standoff has lead to retaliation by anti-government groups. It has been reported that the bombing of the Edward P. Murrah Building in Oklahoma City, OK was motivated by the Koresh event.

The reason I picked this example is that David Koresh used the Bible to "prove" that he was the "Messiah".

There have been others who have done the same. No doubt there will be more in the years to come. The reason why is because the Holy Scriptures, the Bible, are a compilation of the poetry, letters, history and commandments of God and his people. With them come the chance that someone will take it upon themselves to interpret the Scriptures.

This leads me to my first point in listening to God: Relying upon an interpretation of the Bible through an individual is

dangerous. God has come to speak to his people through a written word that is interpreted by his community of people.

Much like a manual for architects is useless or uninformative unless an architect interprets the manual for us, the faith specific terms of the scriptures need interpretation within a community that understands the faith language it contains. It is dangerous for people outside the community of faith to think that they can interpret the Bible without a community of faith.

Every church, whether Catholic, United Methodist, Baptist, Missionary, Mennonite, etc. has a way to interpret the Scriptures. The one thing they all agree on is what is said by St. Paul to St. Timothy, "All Scripture is inspired by God and profitable for teaching, for reproof, for correction, and for training in righteousness, that the man of God may be complete, equipped for every good work."[9]

This passage tells us that the Scriptures were inspired by God to speak to people. The theme is to be spiritual: being in relationship and conversation with God. There is no denomination of Christianity which denies that in some way the Scriptures are the Word of God.

Those of the Anglican and Methodist persuasion say that the Bible is the Word of God in that "all things necessary to salvation are contained therein."[10] Others, such as Baptists

---

[9] RSV, 2 Timothy 3.16

[10] *Articles of Religion*, Anglican Article VI, Methodist Article V.

and fundamentalists, often claim that it is the inerrant word of God that has been handed to us.[11] Catholics believe that "In Sacred Scripture, the Church constantly finds her nourishment and her strength, for she welcomes it not as a human word, but as what it really is, the word of God."[12] The belief is commonly held that the Bible is God's communication to us.

Again, to remain in contact with God, we read the Scriptures within a community of faith.

Some churches say that the Bible is free to anyone's interpretation. Ironically, these communities often have a strict understanding of what the Scriptures say and will not tolerate individual deviation from the communal interpretation.

My understanding of how to interpret the Bible is found in Acts 8. In Acts 8, while Philip was going to Jerusalem from Gaza, as directed by an angel of the Lord, he encounters an Ethiopian Eunuch who is reading a passage from the prophet Isaiah. When Philip approached the chariot in which the Eunuch was riding, he asked, "Do you understand what you are reading?"[13]

The Ethiopian replied, "How can I, unless someone guides

---

[11] *Chicago Statement of Inerrancy*, 1978.

[12] *Catechism of the Catholic Church, para. 104.*

[13] Acts 8.30.

me?"[14] Here is an example of how the guidance of the community of faith is needed to understand the Scriptures. This is important because it is the community of faith that compiled these Scriptures into a "Bible."[15] The Apostle St. Philip is the member of the faith community who guides the Ethiopian Eunuch.

Over time there were any number of "scriptures" that were floating around Christianity. Some were more beneficial than others. Bishops met to choose which ones were really the inspired word of God. It was the community of faith in the beginning which understood that God was speaking through the selected letters and books to the Community.

These books were to be considered as a whole. That is why they were compiled into one source. This seems too simple, but it is true. The books of the Bible were compiled so that they would be considered as a whole.

Some churches pay homage to the Gospels a little more than the others because they contain the words of Jesus Christ, but for the most part, they are considered with equal weight.

It would be unfair to a piece of literature to open it up in the middle read a sentence or two and say you understand the whole story, wouldn't it? So why do we do it to the Bible? The Bible is a story which has a beginning, middle and end. Like a story, we look back on the whole story and gain a

---

[14]Acts 8.31.

[15]Synods of Hippo and Carthage, 393 A.D. and 397 A.D..

fuller understanding of the story when we are done by knowing the conclusion.

The Bible concludes with the coming of Jesus Christ a second time. Like a good novel, we understand the ending better with Jesus Christ as the interpretive key. That understanding of Jesus Christ is at the heart of how a community interprets Scripture.

The other day, a Jehovah's Witness gave me one of their Bibles as a going away present. I opened it up to the Gospel of St. John and it said that "the Word was *a* god." I was horrified. If this is true, it means that there is more than one God. This means that there is a limitation on Jesus Christ, as God.

My understanding of who the living Jesus Christ is, my spiritual understanding, helped me know that this interpretation of the Scriptures was wrong. I know this is true because I have lived in communities of faith where Jesus Christ has made himself known through the breaking of the Bread and sharing of the Cup.

The Catholic Church has its own catechism (teaching manual). It gives a framework from which we can understand how the Bible tells the story. Other churches have their own "Articles of Religion" or "Confession of Faith". All in all, if you know the *Apostle's Creed* or the *Nicene Creed*, then you know the story of the Bible. Read the Bible with these truths in mind.

What does your church or former church say about the

reading and understanding of the Scriptures? You need to know. What a faith-filled community has to say is more important than what an individual has to say. Check it out. That is your assignment for this week.

Assignment

Call your present or former church and ask them to send you an official copy of how your church says you ought to read and understand the Bible.

Read the following copies of the Apostle's and Nicene Creeds.

The Apostle's Creed

I believe in God, the Father Almighty, the Creator of heaven and earth,
and in Jesus Christ, His only Son, our Lord:
Who was conceived of the Holy Spirit, born of the Virgin Mary,
suffered under Pontius Pilate, was crucified, died, and was buried. He descended into hell.

The third day He arose again from the dead.
He ascended into heaven and sits at the right hand of God the Father Almighty,
whence He shall come to judge the living and the dead.

I believe in the Holy Spirit, the holy catholic church,
the communion of saints, the forgiveness of sins,
the resurrection of the body, and life everlasting.

Amen.

The Nicene Creed

We believe in one God, the Father, the Almighty, maker of heaven and earth, of all that is, seen and unseen.

We believe in one Lord, Jesus Christ, the only Son of God, eternally begotten of the Father, God from God, Light from Light, true God from true God, begotten, not made, of one Being with the Father. Through him all things were made. For us and for our salvation he came down from heaven: by the power of the Holy Spirit he became incarnate from the Virgin Mary, and was made man. For our sake he was crucified under Pontius Pilate; he suffered death and was buried. On the third day he rose again in accordance with the Scriptures; he ascended into heaven and is seated at the right hand of the Father. He will come again in glory to judge the living and the dead, and his kingdom will have no end.

We believe in the Holy Spirit, the Lord, the giver of life, who proceeds from the Father. With the Father and the Son he is worshiped and glorified. He has spoken through the Prophets. We believe in one holy catholic and apostolic Church. We acknowledge one baptism for the forgiveness of sins. We look for the resurrection of the dead, and the life of the world to come. Amen.

LESSON 8

How to use a Prayer Book.

Imagine my surprise to open up a January 2000 issue of *Christianity Today* only to find an article on how Evangelicals are using prayer books because they are tired of having to make everything up as they go along! A long sentence, I know, but what a thought! We can become more spiritual by being a little more structured in our prayer time. Prayer books offer that structure. Here is some advice on how to use a prayer book.

Now that we have established a spiritual life, now what? After a routine prayer time, silence, reading scripture, and praying, there is a way to make our spiritual lives better. The answer is in not having to reinvent the wheel. This is the genius of a prayer book.

Prayer Books are simply a compilation of scripture and prayers in an ordered form. Many evangelicals are experiencing what serious Catholics have known for centuries: meditating on Scripture in small doses is a wonderful way to start, continue and end the day.

Prayer Books usually have one basic pattern which you follow. It is called "the Ordinary". This is the format of how your prayer time is outlined by the prayer book. It will simply tell you, "Pray first, sing a hymn now, read a passage of scripture now, end here."

Most prayer books have sections for prayers for the particular

week of the Christian calendar. These prayers are usually called "Collect(s)". Think of them simply as "collecting" the thoughts and intentions of the day.

The Psalms are next. The Psalms were the first hymns sung by the Hebrew people and then by Christians. They are the "first Scriptures" for the first Christians. We covered the Psalms in the first lessons of this book.

There are usually shorter forms and longer forms of prayer books. There are several options.

A Small Meal

For those who are caught up in the hectic world of the "Information Age" it might be easier to handle getting spiritual in small bites. These are prayer books with an outline for prayer time that are small, usually ten to fifteen minutes in length.

The Shorter Christian Prayer is a must have for all lay Catholics and for those who are learning. A companion book *School of Prayer* tells you what is going on blow by blow in Shorter Christian Prayer.

Shorter Christian Prayer has the Ordinary at the beginning and gives you the outline. After this ordinary will follow four weeks of Morning and Evening Prayer forms for each day for a month. This is called "the four-week cycle." This four-week cycle takes you through a good many of the Psalms.

This book is designed for you to say prayers before work,

after work and at bedtime in short ten to fifteen minute increments. After the four-week cycle, there is a section called "Night Prayer" which is said on a weekly cycle. Be sure to say a prayer of confession before you start each night.

Another Small Meal

The Book of Common Prayer, page 137, has an ordinary with everything in it. It is designed for "Families and Individuals". It tells you what needs to be done daily, but doesn't change much. It is the same form for each time of the day for prayer. You can look in the different sections of The Book of Common Prayer to find a different Psalm, different Collect, different prayer of confession, etc. You are left largely to yourself to fill in the blanks of the Ordinary.

There are larger Ordinary's in *The Book of Common Prayer*, but they are largely the same: you need to carry around another book or two to be able to finish your prayer time.

Other Small Meals

Daily Prayer 2009. You can use other popular prayer books to help you. Liturgical Training Press out of Chicago offers *Daily Prayer [year number, i.e. "2009"]*. This is a tremendous book. It has everything laid out for you on a daily basis. It comes with a reflection on the scriptures for that day. You will need to purchase this book yearly.

Magnificat is a monthly prayer book that has the *Liturgy of the Hours* already laid out for you. It is published by Magnificat USA of Yonkers, New York.

A Full Meal
A truly full meal for those with a strong spiritual hunger can be found in *The Liturgy of the Hours.* This is the Roman Catholic four volume prayer book, and man is it serious! Chock full of Scripture and prayers written by faithful people, *The Liturgy of the Hours'* four volumes each cover one or two 'seasons' of the Christian Year. You will need to know the "Liturgical Calendar" to understand where you are and where to go next.

There are seasons to the Christian year. Each season focuses on certain aspects of the Christian life we should be living all the time.

The purpose of the Christian Year is twofold. First, it allows us to focus on the things we ought to be doing without being overwhelmed by the whole thing. Secondly, the Christian Year allows us to focus on parts of Christ's life as we remember that he was born of the Virgin Mary, suffered under Pontius Pilate, was crucified, died and buried. On the third day, he rose from the dead, ascended into heaven and is seated at the right hand of the Father--whew!

Each volume of The Liturgy of the Hours has basically the same set up. The one volume for Advent is set up a little differently because it doesn't cover as many days as the others. Yet, the format is usually like this:

1. Scripture Readings and readings by the Church Fathers for the day.
2. The Ordinary.
3. The Four Week Cycle of Reading, Morning Prayer,

Daytime Prayer, Evening Prayer and Night Prayer (nine times per day in all).
4. Different patterns of prayer for special days, called the "Common". You use these if you follow the days of the Saints.
5. Readings for the special days.

For those interested in learning how to use this wonderful mammoth of a prayer book, contact me at mark@myspiritualadvisor.com for suggestions and lessons.

Closing Thoughts on Prayer Books

Whatever prayer book you choose, please be sure that the prayer book includes readings from the Bible. It is critical that reading the Scriptures are our connection to Christ.

LESSON 9

Why Church

Last year, according to a magazine account, a twelve-year old boy committed suicide. Why did he do it? He did it because all of the children at school were making fun of him because of the way he smelled. According to the magazine's sources, he had no friends at school. He was truly alone. Being alone is one of the things that God really doesn't want for any of us.

One of the things you do not read in the newspapers about being in relationship with God is that there is not just a connection to this Person, but there is a connection to other people. When you become more spiritual you are never really alone. When you become spiritual, you are connected in a very real and very deep way with other people all over the world.

I only wish that the young man who killed himself last year would have known that becoming spiritual comes with a family that can make up for how cruel the world can be. When you become spiritual there should be a deeper connection to other people. This doesn't mean that you can stop everyone from hurting themselves, but you can encourage people out of a lonely state of mind.

The Holy Scriptures say, "for in Christ Jesus you are all sons of God, through faith. For as many of you as were baptized into Christ have put on Christ . There is neither Jew nor Greek, there is neither slave nor free, there is neither male

nor female; for you are all one in Christ Jesus. And if you are Christ's, then you are Abraham's offspring, heirs according to promise."[16]

Christians believe that baptism actually makes us part of Jesus Christ. Because God is Spirit, he can connect us spiritually in Jesus Christ. This is not just a spiritual connection. Christians believe that we are connected physically by Jesus. We are connected to him physically and spiritually in the meal of his body and blood in the Eucharist. This physical connection is entered into in Baptism.

Because of this connection, "If one member suffers, all suffer together; if one member is honored, all rejoice together. Now you are the body of Christ and individually members of it."[17] There is a communal aspect of becoming more spiritual.

This aspect of spirituality is why we need to be together as a group. That group is called "church". What we share in common is being made a part of Christ. This bond draws us together to help each other. It means that when we feel like we want to die, we can have peace because we have friends. In fact, we have an obligation to remain alive and thrive so that we can build up the community.

Being a member of the church means we have a group of people who will love us, even if they don't like us or the way

---

[16]Galatians 3.26-29.

[17]1 Corinthians 12.26-27.

we smell. There may be people who don't understand this great mystery, but there will be at least one to two people who understand that we mean a great deal to each other when we become more spiritual.

Once you get there, what happens during the church service or Mass?

It might be helpful to understand what is going on at a church service or Mass when you arrive at a Christian or Catholic Church. What happens is really very simple.

Simply put, you will "connect with God" in a deeper way by gathering with other members of the church. When you walk into a Mass, in particular, you will be with people who have been spiritual for as many as fifty years or more. They have had a deep relationship with God. Hopefully, the church will have a time after the church service or Mass when you can meet these good people and get to know about their lives.

There are four parts to a church service or Mass. These parts are *The Entrance/Introductory Rites*, *The Service of the Word*, *The Service of the Eucharist,* and *The Sending Forth/Concluding Rites/Benediction.*

The Entrance or Introductory Rites

Imagine if we greeted each other by asking each other to forgive our neglect and ways that we hurt each other. There would be many better relationships in our lives. Many people who start a spiritual life are sorry that they did not recognize God was the one working in their lives. This part of the

Mass/Service gives us a chance to begin or renew that relationship.

The Entrance/Introductory Rites is the first part of the service or Mass. The entrance basically says, "we are all gathered here in the name of God: Father, Son and Holy Spirit." We greet the Person with whom we are becoming more spiritual. We greet him by saying, "I am sorry if I have neglected you or made you angry." What is wonderful is that God says back to us through the priest/pastor, "I forgive you. Forget it. Let's renew our relationship."

The Service of the Word

The Service of the Word is the second part of the Mass. It is the part where we hear the word of God which has been spoken to us for millennia. Along with that ancient proclamation is an application of that word to us for today. The ancient proclamation is from the Holy Scriptures of the Bible. The application of the word for us today is called a Homily or Sermon.

This section ends with us responding to these proclamations with two parts. The first part says, "We hear it and we believe it." It is called the "Creed." It is a group statement of belief which is almost as old as the church itself. It is a way for us to celebrate our common bond. There is also a group prayer to God so that we can share our common concerns with God, anticipating God's blessing and remedy. Don't worry about knowing it when you first visit. You can find copies of this creed in the song book in front of you.

The Eucharist/Service of the Table

The Eucharist/Service of the Table is the climax of our lives. What happens is that Jesus Christ (the Son of "Father, Son and Holy Spirit") has found a way to share with us through our physical nature.

We Christians make an outrageous claim. We claim that we become more spiritual by doing something physical. We claim that Jesus Christ makes the bread and the wine his resurrected, physical body. We become more spiritual by eating it. This makes the Spirit enter into us in a most physical way.

The Eucharist/Service of the Table starts with the giving of bread and wine which is placed on the altar. The priest/pastor calls everyone to the table just like dinner at home. He asks the Holy Spirit to change the bread and the wine. We believe something incredible happens: the bread is incorporated into the physical body of Jesus Christ in the heavens. When that happens, we are truly spiritual through the physical.

It is important to know that those who are connected to Christ through baptism are welcomed to the table to eat. Those who have just discovered spirituality are encouraged to receive a blessing and wait until they have developed and formalized their relationship with Father, Son and Holy Spirit to eat. This is just like we have discussed previously, we need to be patient with ourselves and let things develop.

The Benediction is the last part of the Service/Mass. It is

where we are sent forth to be spiritual beings through our physical bodies in the world. Although we say good bye to some of our new brothers and sisters for the moment, we also anticipate meeting with them and God again next week.

Assignment

Find out the times Mass/Worship Service starts at several churches, including a Catholic Church. Attend one or more for the next four weeks. Give the churches that catch your attention four weeks before you decide which one you feel you should join.

Lesson 10

Do I Really Need to Join a Church?

In attempting to give spiritual advice to the world there is a problem. In giving advice at my website, MySpiritualAdvisor.com we find that the world at large, well, it has "issues" with God.

The major barrier for the world to "become more spiritual" has been a HUGE distrust of God. The world seems to be saying loudly and clearly that they can't stand God. But the question we haven't asked up to this point is this: Can God stand us?

I remember a choir director I had said to me, "If it weren't for Jesus Christ, we wouldn't be speaking to each other." I agreed, we would not love each other if it weren't for Jesus Christ. Sad to say, but there are people at church who really grate on everyone's nerves (I hope it isn't me!). There is no getting around it. It seems that the world would be perfect if it just didn't have people (me included).

There is no getting around people. They are simply everywhere. This seems to be another major impediment to wanting to join a church.

In the preceding lessons, we have talked about the spiritual nature of God. He is the only thing that can fill our empty void. He reaches out to us through Jesus Christ. He loves us.

Let’s do a little spiritual exercise which will drive home the fact that God loves us. First, close your eyes (after you get done reading this). Then imagine the most irritating person in your entire world. Then think about this: God loves them. Now that you have picked yourself up off the floor, let’s think about this: You may very well be a person that someone else has imagined when doing this exercise.

With all of the little fights we pick and things we won’t forget, it is amazing that God wants to have anything to do with us. So, if one of our objections to joining the church is the people, then we are simply not spiritual. If being spiritual is doing what Jesus Christ (who is spirit become flesh) does, then we must seek out other people throughout our lives, no matter how irritating people might be.

Not only does God love them, he became one of them. Believe you me. Jesus Christ irritated quite a few people. He irritated them so much that they decided to kill him. He died willingly because he loved them. He died even for the irritating people.

In the Mass at the Catholic Church I am attending are these words, "Lord, look not upon our sins, but upon the faith of your church." These words are key to becoming more spiritual.

The best spiritual advice is based on the understanding that there is something more out there. There is a higher calling than to just "unleash the power within." Why would I want to "unleash" me without change when the "me" I am is not getting it done? There is more to the picture.

There is a relationship with someone who is otherworldly, beyond our reach. That one, named Father, Son and Holy Spirit, is the one who comes to us and others. It is all about uniting with each other as we unite through him, with him, and in him.

Jesus Christ's resurrection achieves a pathway for us to become one with him. He showed that the way to the Spirit is through commitment. We need to follow the example and become committed to him. God does not want so much for us to be happy as he wants us to be committed to him. This commitment comes when we are committed to those who are also committed to him.

Rather than quoting Bible verses, let me make a point about when Jesus Christ walked the earth. When Jesus started his ministry, he gathered people to him. He went out and picked the Twelve Apostles. He didn't sit in his room alone. He didn't eat alone. He didn't go to the record store on Friday Night, get some carry out food and then go home for the evening alone. When Christ came, he formed a community.

To that community, he was committed. He taught them. He took them all over Palestine. He shared his thoughts and visions of a new world order, a new covenant with humanity. Here is another observation: he was so committed that he gave his own life for the cause.

Through a spiritual bond formed in Christian Baptism, we become one with Christ. Through this mysterious spiritual union, we become part of Christ. When Christ died, we

died. When Christ rose from the dead, we rose from the dead. When Christ goes to heaven, we go to heaven.

Not only do we personally do these things, but everyone else who loves Christ and is baptized does the same thing. Joining the people who are committed to Christ cements the message that we send to God. Becoming more spiritual means that we do what God does. God is committed to the point of death for his people and all the world, and we need to be committed to that group of people as well.

We show our commitment to God by joining in a public way with the others who openly love him. To NOT join a church is like living with someone without commitment. Living together is a cheap way to use another human being. It is a way to get all of the benefits without paying the price.

Going to church without joining is using God to make ourselves feel better without having to acknowledge the claim that God has on our lives. My advice is to join a church.

Here is how to join church:
Attend a church for at least four Sundays to see if it is a place you would like to investigate. Ask for literature to read about what the church believes. Ask some people what is the best thing about their church to see if faith, God and the mission of God are central to their life. Meet with the pastor/priest. If you can't get an appointment with the Pastor/Priest, or you can't get in for a long time, then you should go somewhere else. The church may be big enough to have another staff member or another minister/priest meet with you. This is fine. The objective is to find out if you will be

cared for in the long run.

Assignment

Decide that you are going to take at least three months to choose a church. Find out where some people you know go to church and attend with them. Go at least four times to each church. Ask for the information I mentioned above and then make an appointment with the pastor, priest or staff member so they can tell you about their church.

Lesson 11

Do I Really Need to Receive Holy Communion?

Did you know that a baby will die if it is not given affection? There is a reason why, and in your quest to become more spiritual you are fulfilling that common need for affection. Way back when we started this little project to give advice to those starving for spiritual insights, be them pagan, protestant or Catholic, we were all longing for "somethin'".

Back then, my advice was that this desire to not be alone, not be depressed or not be lost was a search for God. This is good advice. But this quest for the spiritual you and I are on is more than just a quest to know God, it is a spiritual quest for another something.

Could you imagine a baby surviving by himself? Who would feed her? Who would teach him how to communicate? Who would provide for her needs? The idea of a baby living by himself from the start is ludicrous. This physical reality has a spiritual reality that is tied to it.

For today, we will concentrate on three ways that Holy Communion unites us. There are more, but space will not permit. The three ways that Holy Communion unites us are the following:

Holy Communion unites us with God.
Holy Communion unites us with each other.
Holy Communion unites us with forgiveness.

All of these things come from being in community with each other and with Jesus Christ in the receiving of his body and blood.

Just like a baby needs to have a mother and a father provide for her needs, a human being has a need to be in community with others. Oh, sure, there are exceptions to the rule, but the underlying truth is that "it is not good for man to be alone." We are social beings. Even the best hermit relied on a small community of two or three to get her to the point where she could ignore the rest of the world.

Just before the birth of our fifth child, we needed to decide living arrangements and make the necessary accommodations (which is a fancy way of saying, "Where are we going to put this kid?"). We decided that the new baby would share a room with our fourth child.

We began the task of moving things around to fit a crib, etc. That is when our then three-year-old son looked up with wonderment and a gleam in his eye and said, "Are *we* getting *my* room ready for *our* baby?"

Besides my heart filling with joy, and my eyes with tears, it was a wonderful moment that my son realized that his soon to be sister was his. We all belong to each other. The central truth of "loving our neighbor as ourselves" is that we belong to each other in God.

In Genesis, chapter 4, Cain killed his brother Abel out of selfish ambition and disregard for anyone's life but his own. The text tells us that Cain and Abel made offerings to the

Lord. When Cain's offering wasn't as good as Abel's, Cain was enraged. The easiest target of his ambition filled rage was his brother. After killing his brother, he felt he had to defend himself before God. When asked where Abel had gone, Cain replied, "Am I my brother's keeper?"

For years, I have asked people if we Christians have a responsibility to be our brother's keeper. There is only one an answer to this question. That answer is, "YES! You are your brother's keeper." We do have a responsibility to tend to the life of our brother and sister. This is at the heart of being a Christian.

The need to satisfy that empty space in you is only found in God and loving your neighbor. Nowhere else are these two needs more fully met than in participating in the event Christians call "Holy Communion" or the "Eucharist."

Holy Communion is a meal that bridges gaps. There used to be a gap between God in the heavens and humanity on earth. When we take the body of Christ (the bread) into our hands and then ingest him in our mouths, we are bringing the Divine to earth and into our own bodies. This means we bridge the gap between humanity and the Divine. Now that is becoming more spiritual!

It is a meal that bridges the gap between peoples. (See Romans 6). Those who are baptized are literally baptized into the life of Christ, into his body. The meal we take from one loaf or one batch of wafers is a living symbol of the fact that we are one in Jesus Christ. In a previous lesson we talked about the people at church who drive us crazy. Holy

Communion is a common uniting with Christ that crosses over all things that would keep us away from each other.

By becoming more spiritual, we cross over the lines that divide us by uniting in Jesus Christ. To turn the phrase 'unity in diversity' on its head, Holy Communion is diversity in unity. Becoming more spiritual in Holy Communion also takes care of all those ways we miss the mark and disappoint God through the mean and forgetful things we do.

For anyone who has seen Mel Gibson's film, "The Passion of the Christ," you can see that Jesus was executed in a bloody sacrifice on the cross. The Crucifixion is a culmination of several biblical passages. These passages all lead to a common understanding: Jesus Christ was giving his innocent life on the Cross willingly for the sins of the world.

The passages that come together are: Exodus 12 and 16, Leviticus 1, John 1.29-34 and 6.25-59, Mark 14.12-26, Acts 2.42. All of these trace a path that leads us to understand the "it" is Jesus Christ who is offered for our sins. In Holy Communion that forgiveness achieved on the Cross is given to us in the bread and the cup.

Rather than giving advice that commands us to receive Holy Communion, I will ask some simple questions. Do you want to be united with the spiritual Divinity? Do you want to live in a community where people are united? Do you want to be forgiven of your wrongs and sins? If so, then why wouldn't you want to receive Holy Communion? Case closed.

When we are united with Christ in Holy Communion, it is then that the child can look at his room and share it with *our* baby. It is then that we can forgive others who have wronged us and God. It is then that we can truly become more spiritual as we encounter Jesus' body and blood.

Assignment
Do whatever it takes in your new church to be able to receive the Eucharist/Holy Communion.

